Into the Bardo

Into the Bardo

Poems by

Jim Miller

© 2024 Jim Miller. All rights reserved.
This material may not be reproduced in any form, published,
reprinted, recorded, performed, broadcast,
rewritten, or redistributed without
the explicit permission of Jim Miller.
All such actions are strictly prohibited by law.

Cover design by Shay Culligan
Cover image by Perry Vasquez
Author photo by Kelly Mayhew

ISBN: 978-1-63980-639-3
Library of Congress Control Number: 2024945871

Kelsay Books
502 South 1040 East, A-119
American Fork, Utah 84003
Kelsaybooks.com

For Walter

Acknowledgments

I would like to thank my first editor-in-chief, Kelly Mayhew, for her thorough evaluation and editing of this text. My eternal gratitude is also extended to Alys Masek, Hector Martinez, and Manuel Paul López for their painstaking edits and evaluation of the book. Thanks as well to Kendra Tanacea for her insightful feedback and blurb. And much gratitude to Perry Vasquez for his evocative cover art. This chapbook would never have happened without them.

Finally, I would be remiss if I did not thank my best friend, Ben Garrett, M.D., whose medical advice and help saved my life along with the excellent care of the surgical team and nurses at the Jacobs Medical Center at the University of California, San Diego and the doctors and staff at Kaiser Permanente San Diego. I would not have lived to recount my experience were it not for all of them. There is no way I will ever be able to repay this debt or the debt I owe to the stranger whose liver donation gave me a second chance at life.

Contents

Preface: Enter the Bardo	13
In Kihei, Late June 2023	17
Grace	18
The Imperfect Now	20
Where Despair Lives	22
Naked	23
The Glory of Love	24
Traces	25
The Day I Found Out	26
Into the Bardo	27
The Things We Carry	30
Lost	35
Rage	37
A Tale of Two Cities	38
Crown of Thorns	40
Stars	42
The Big Dance	45
What Was It Like?	49
Gift	54
This One Small Life	55

It's good to be alive
It's good to be alive
It's good to know we die
It's good to know

Infinite surprise
Infinite surprise
Infinite surprise

—Wilco, "Infinite Surprise"

Preface: Enter the Bardo

In the summer of 2023, I was diagnosed with acute, sudden liver failure, had transplant surgery, a neurotoxic reaction to one of my anti-rejection medications, and multiple near-death experiences.

Tibetan Buddhist nun, Pema Chödrön, in her book *How We Live Is How We Die,* defines the states of being I inhabited as a kind of "bardo" or transition, which comes from the *Bardo Tödrol* or *The Tibetan Book of the Dead.*

As Chödrön observes, the term bardo, "commonly refers to the passage following our death and preceding our next life." She goes on to say:

> . . . a broader translation of the word is simply "transition" or "gap." The journey that takes place after our death is one such transition, but when we examine our experience closely, we will find that we are always in transition. During every moment of our lives, something is ending and something else is beginning. This is not an esoteric concept. When we pay attention, it becomes our unmistakable experience.

Bardos, then, are states of "continual change," a "continual flow of transitions" from one thing to another.

I was dying. And then I wasn't. Now I am aware that, even with new medications to control the worst of my symptoms and make sure my body doesn't reject my new liver, for the rest of my life, every moment is tentative and precious. The future is always uncertain, becoming and ending and becoming again.

As Chödrön shows us, although "we are not in control" and are forced by circumstance to recognize that "stable, solid reality is an illusion," what the bardo teachings illustrate, according to her, is that deeply engaging with "impermanence" and "all pervasive suffering" does not inevitably lead to despair but puts us face to face with the "wonderous flow of life and death." Seeing this flow at the center of a universe where "everything falls apart" enables us to admire the joy and beauty at the heart of the dance of life and death. We can stop our constant running away from and resisting reality and adopt "a new way of seeing our [lives] as dynamic and vibrant, an amazing adventure."

I lived and am living this.

The first several poems that comprise this collection were written before my formal diagnosis when I began to feel that I was very sick and was dealing with a profound sense of doom. They document that moment when one construct I had of myself was annihilated as everything was torn asunder, and I was forced into the uncertainty of the bardo as I had to accept a disconcerting reality and see what remained of my existence anew.

Also included here are poems from June 25, 2023 until my liver transplant a month later. My transplant operation barely came in time to save my life, and thus resulted in my first near-death experience. I wrote about that soon after my surgery in a column I published in the *San Diego Union-Tribune,* where I observed that:

> The great James Baldwin's title character in "Sonny's Blues" says that sometimes you need to "smell your own stink." I did. I was incredibly humbled, made aware of the lack of control I had over things we delude ourselves we

can control. I watched my body and my mind's decline—I had lost my ability to read deeply, to write and even to think clearly by the time I reached the operation table. My idea of "me" withered, and I was not at all confident I would be there after the surgery. I had to tell the ones I love the most, my son, my wife, my family, my closest friends, that I might not make it out of the operation room, the kinds of conversations I would wish on no one, friend or foe.

Thus, a number of the poems in this book deal with the surgery and its immediate aftermath, while the remaining works address the horrific side effects to one of the medications I was prescribed that led to neurotoxicity and a host of jarring physical and psychological consequences. Hence came another series of dark nights of the soul, which I gradually made my way through only to be hit with an undiagnosed lung infection two months later that left me coughing up blood and put me in the hospital for yet another week as I endured new tests and invasive procedures before my turn for the better.

It was only the love of my family, friends, and community that helped me down this path. In addition to that, my adherence to my own idiosyncratic version of Buddhist discipline and an existential effort to maintain some form of grace under pressure were essential tools for my recovery and redemption. The tale of this journey is ongoing but my experience to date has taught me that it is in these interstices, these bardos of our lives, whether they be painful, joyous, or uncertain and bittersweet, that we are most fully alive.

Sometimes it is only by being shattered that we are truly set free.

In Kihei, Late June 2023

Sometimes it makes its way through tears.
After a season of dread and trembling,
you go straight to it,
diving into the heart of your shattered self and beyond it,
to the sound of roosters crowing at dawn
mixing with the rhythmic chants of the crews
on the outrigger canoes offshore,
the smell of coffee brewing,
and the sweet lull of the morning sea.
There is nothing on the far horizon but endless blue.
And then, suddenly, it is silent.
Anything can happen, even now.

Grace

In the wake of so many losses,
day after day of
pain, decline, enervation,
abandonment, absence,
and soul-crushing angst,
I am destroyed.
Somewhere in the wreckage of myself,
a deep yearning persists,
like a sweet melancholy voice in a long-forgotten song.
There are stars behind the clouds,
and lush green fields of memory.

My lover's voice whispers
the promise of a tender, poignant,
no, sacred,
moment yet to be—
dazzling sunlight dancing on the water.
Around the corner,
there is a road
that leads to a place where all is beloved,
and under the shade of ancient redwoods
by a murmuring creek,
sorrow gives way to joy,
and the shadow of death
surrenders to an ethereal light.

I remember a time when the beautiful
was not always colored by the looming threat
of the end of things,
when to live was to live—unhindered.

Now it is only your tender lips,
your caress,
and lovely, bright green eyes
that pull me back to the struggle
to live in the world,
moment by moment,
breath by breath,
groping for just one instance
of grace.

The Imperfect Now

Trembling in paradise,
I sit on a chair in the shade
looking out the window
at the expanse of green green grass,
rolling toward the silver road of the sun
glittering on the deep blue ocean.

There is nothing left anymore.
No dreams of a brighter future,
no roads yet to be taken.
Just this imperfect now,
the cool breeze on my face,
a catamaran in the distance,
with its white sails pushing on
against the rising waves.
The palm trees are bowing to the wind,
and the sound of ceaseless surf
is operatic.

My body aches in a thousand places,
and the nausea is raging within
but my eyes still take delight
in tender glimpses of the radiant world—
a turtle's head pops up and gasps for air,
and the silhouette of the frozen lava flow
is framed by the boundless sea.

I should drown myself in this
pain and longing,
and be reborn diffuse,
surging and flowing,
from matter to emptiness,

part of the nothing
that is inside
the billowing clouds
that aimlessly roam the sky
and make the poetry of the day's last light
sing
before it dies gently
in the darkness
like the first words of a prayer.

Where Despair Lives

Despair lives in the blood red heart of the sunset,
waiting for the loneliest moment.
It is mocked by the trailing sounds
of children playing in the distance,
and it comingles with the subtle,
yet luminous pink of the cloud-shrouded twilight,
and knows that the darkness to follow
is really just a pause before the dawn
that it will never have the pleasure of greeting.

Naked

We wake from restless sleep
in the pitch dark,
sweating, hearts racing,
our two heads spinning
in their own separate hells,
helplessly charting the waters
of uncertainty and fear
in the long shadow
of my possible end.
I can hear you quietly weeping,
and I search for your hand,
and find it, warm and tender,
a naked thing lost in the black night.
We embrace
without words,
and lie together, breathing deeply,
desperately hoping for the release of slumber.
Slowly, in unison, we drift off,
as if dying, blissfully,
in the arms of a love
beyond desire.

The Glory of Love

This is what sustains me:
our lives are a choice,
as Aldous Huxley once wrote,
between love and freedom.
And when you choose love,
a part of yourself dies,
chained forever to grief, suffering, and loss.
You are redeemed only by
losing yourself in the eyes of your lover,
and finding the child of that love
is a vast universe
of wonder and discovery
who connects you, simultaneously,
to the lives of those who came before you,
and the lives of those yet to be born.

In that stark otherness,
the world is reborn,
and you wander there,
humble and full of awe at the simplest occurrences—
the crispness of winter,
the verdant smell of spring,
the moist, humid air of summer,
a slant of fall light.

All of these things
keep you wondering
at how small you are—
one part of some vast,
ungainly, gorgeous beast,
that you'll never
understand.

Traces

Staying in his future grandchild's room,
perhaps my brother, the eldest sibling of my family,
ponders whether this will be the last time
he has a place in his daughter's house.
Maybe, rather than a beginning,
it is the end of his time.

And it's true that after giving so much,
we all come to a place where we wonder,
what have I done in this one,
precious life?
Will all the memories of cold metal bleachers at ballgames
and hikes in the rocky, pine-scented woods
endure from my child to theirs?
What good are the traces of love that we leave to linger
before they disappear into the dark forest of the past?
I think of my son
and hope that I will be held dear
in his memory
as my ashes
flow down the river to
the thick, salty waters of the sea
to join the atoms of
my parents and theirs before them
forever flowing,
lost beyond time.

The Day I Found Out

After the doctor's call
brought me the bad news,
I drove through town, then walked down the beach
like a looming dark cloud, despite the luminous day
and the sparkling light on the ocean.
I was lost in petty thoughts and bitterness.
How could this befall me?

I went on this way, ignoring the stunningly red rooster
strutting by the bushes
near our place.
I was deaf to the birdsong bursting from trees.
It was only as I started climbing the stairs to the second floor
that I stopped and noticed a gecko on the rail
and leaned over to inspect its
delicate emerald body
and strange round eyes,
frozen there for a minute as if to say,
"Hello, dear friend."
I put my hand down slowly to touch it,
but the gecko wisely scurried away,
and disappeared around the corner.

When I looked up,
the blazing sun was dancing on the distant, azure sea,
beckoning me
to stop clinging to my suffering
and come back to myself
that very instant.

Why not me, after all?

Into the Bardo

after Pema Chödrön

During the dawning hours,
I struggled to sleep,
failing to catch even
a stray minute of peace.
Throughout it all
my nurse, Jeff, said to me,
in his calm, steady voice,
"Go with the river,
you can't fight the river,
go with the river."
He repeated it, over and over,
like a mantra,
and his words stayed with me
throughout the night,
into the early morning
and onward to this day.

Before they came to take me to surgery,
I said to my son, "If I don't make it, remember to
look at your hand and I'll be there, always."
My wife wiped away my tears, kissed me,
and, as they wheeled me down the hallway,
I recalled what I told my son the day before,
as I cradled his head in my hands,
"Be not afraid, have courage, and be steadfast."

But in my gut, I was sure I would die.

Death was smiling at me in the darkness,
waiting patiently by my side,
whispering to me that
it was time to pass over,

quietly and quickly,
to his lonely kingdom.

"It will be a delicate and difficult procedure,"
I heard a surgeon say in the operating room,
thinking that I had already gone under.

So, I lay there, on the razor's edge.
Now, I knew I had
no time, no time, no time
to waste—

Not. One. Moment. More.

My body had been screaming this for months,
and now the doctors knew it too
as they spoke in a semi-whisper,
"Let's start the procedure."
As the anesthesia took hold,
I occupied a space between life and death,
tiptoeing along the border,
trying to impose a semblance of order
on my inner chaos.
I held tightly to the discipline of
just breathing in and out,
in and out,
deeply and slowly,
and letting whatever came to be
sit there as it was.

Suddenly, I reached a strange state
of grace
and went blank.

My last thought,
before the six-hour caesura,
was of teaching Hemingway's
"A Clean Well-Lighted Place"
in a classroom with a view
of a distant tree
shedding a few
reluctant autumn leaves
in the soft breeze.

And then deep nothingness, suspended from time.

Still lying on my back,
I came back to consciousness,
furtively, eyes closed,
silently repeating to myself
a line from Pema Chödrön,
"How we live is how we die,"
which I seamlessly replaced
with a memory of my nurse
slowly guiding me forward,
"Don't fight the river, go with it.
You can't fight the river,
let it flow through you."

Amen.

The Things We Carry

after Tim O'Brien

It keeps coming back to me,
the night in the hospital
before my transplant,
laying in the pitch dark,
for what seemed like
an eternity,
breath by breath,
facing the terror,
the sense of doom,
leaning into it
and trying to summon
the courage to bear
the weight of the moment.

In the morning,
I told my son that,
if I died,
he could look at his hand to find me,
and I meant to add,
"because I am you and you are me,"
but I only thought that,
frail and frayed as I was.

Now, in the wake of that visit with near-death,
so many other bleak spaces
have opened up
and the memories, like hungry ghosts,
come flooding back to me—
the time I saw a homeless student
cast off in the gutter,
face down and not breathing
one merciless morning on Broadway.

Working the nightshift
at a dive bar downtown,
back when the streets were
more relentlessly mean,
I saw them.
One poor soul who'd been stabbed, sat lifeless,
in a pool of fresh blood,
up against a wall,
in front of the closed door of a dead hotel.
Another, a woman, slumped over, with blue lips
and a needle in her arm, on the corner just steps away
from the door where I stood watch,
checking IDs,
and looking out
for trouble.

Then there was the man staggering across a vacant lot,
crying for help as he was viciously beaten
by a pack of young boys.

No, the police never came.

And, as if these memories, burned into my brain,
are not enough,
I recall the day when I scrubbed dried blood
from the floor
where my father had fallen
off the toilet,
splitting open his forehead
as he left this world,
alone.

In the sink,
the blood took new life as
I squeezed it out of the sponge,
and it baptized me,
running down the drain,
deep red and
forever squandered,
like the final decades of
my father's life,
drowned in alcohol,
untold sorrow and regret.
His mother had died
when he was only a boy,
lost in a car crash
on a lonely American highway
in the forgotten Midwest of the past.

I remember too, the days
my brother and I spent
clearing out the wreckage of
our mother's house—
old scraps of refuse crumbling in our hands
as we waded through reams of paper
and handwritten notes,
made so she could cling desperately
to the names of her children
and their children
as they continued
to escape her,
drawn back inevitably
into oblivion.
That and the sad discovery of jars of stored feces,

urine-soaked linens,
and putrid couch cushions,
still haunt me
and fill me with
the bottomless grief
of pure loneliness.

Also, branded onto my distant memory,
now pouring back in,
are the days in the wake
of our son's cancer diagnosis,
the numb terror
and unspeakable horror of
imagining the loss
of our only beloved son
at 11-years old—
before his life had a chance
to even begin.

We endured this,
until miraculously
the medication worked
and held his cancer
frozen in check,
but it still lives there,
looming through the years of remission,
making every day we share sacred,
pulsing with meaning, love, and
a trembling tenderness.
He is 19 now, thriving, but this and
everything else we carry,

like so many others—
really everyone, all of us—
make each transient moment
holy and starkly beautiful.

As Gary Snyder once said
to a friend bemoaning
the inevitable slings and arrows of fate,
"Enjoy it while it lasts,"
dive into it, breathe deeply, and feel
the multigrained texture of life
as it flows on ceaselessly
past even death,
into the ocean
of everything that is.

Lost

The monsters came out,
a demon-faced Mara visited for tea,
and my mind turned against me.
I was like the hopeless souls you see
wandering the streets,
raving at someone, something unseen.
I was unmoored.
There were voices in my head,
telling me I was going to suffer,
more and more intensely,
and then die.
Everyone and everything would die.

To combat this,
I made list after list,
desperately took meticulous notes
that no one could read,
did everything I could to make order
out of the burgeoning chaos.
But I failed.

Still somewhere, inside, always,
there was the one who watches,
calmly observing my descent into madness,
bearing witness to
the helpless looks of terror and panic
on the faces of my family.

Then, one night, this happened
while I was trying to watch baseball on TV.
Slowly, it came upon me,
like a fog falling from the sky,

and drifting across a desolate field
or forgotten plain.
No, it was more like a dense, suffocating
wall of whiteness that engulfs
an empty stretch of desert highway
and leaves you suddenly powerless behind the wheel.
I didn't know who I was
and couldn't remember
anything at all.
Lost, utterly lost,
I fell into quicksand,
and the deeper I sank,
the faster the hole filled in
around me,
until nothing was left,
not even a stray memory
to flit across
the screen
before vanishing instantaneously.
My eyes were open
but only as mirrors
to the abyss.

Rage

I was still there, somewhere, seeing it all,
when I lashed out,
pounding the door jamb with both fists,
cursing and raving
in psychotic anger
at those I love the most,
turning our home into a bleak space of dread.

The next day, at the hospital lab,
I saw myself faint
and brace my back against a wall
to slide to the floor
as the staff rushed in
to take me to the ER.
A crowd of onlookers gawked
and pointed,
but I held firm,
clenched my teeth,
pushed them away from my face,
and refused to be taken.

After this, I made a sacred vow to
spare my caretakers
from the worst of me,
but I failed, again and again,
and was ashamed
but still
went on raging, raging, raging
against my
vanishing
self.

A Tale of Two Cities

When the first seizure hit
I flailed and shook
out of control in my chair,
my eyes rolling up in my head.
As I came back to myself,
I could only repeat what was said to me,
like an unctuous parrot performing for snacks.
Ignoring my wife
who they called "hysterical,"
the ambulance crew refused
to take me to the Jacobs Medical Center
where I had been treated before,
delivering me instead
to the emergency room in Hillcrest
where those without my privilege—
the very poor
and people of color
who don't have insurance—
come by necessity.
"You're not in La Jolla anymore," I thought
as I laid on a stretcher and waited
for over an hour
for a spot to open.
Amidst my delirium and episodic bouts of aphasia,
I was placed behind a curtain
in a room with no toilet or water or access to communication
and had another seizure.
The hours from midnight on
were a festival of cruelty and sorrow.
It was, as one friend put it, "like a hospital in hell."
Prone and defeated,

I listened to the understaffed
and burned-out night shift
yell at the homeless,
bully the poor, and
rush folks out the door as soon as they could.
There was no dignity
in this place of last resort.
My wife and I were screamed at
by a voice coming from an in-room speaker
for pushing a button that we never touched.
Only a small number of younger doctors
and nurses were kind enough to
treat their patients with respect and courtesy,
but they were soon rebuffed by their
elder supervisors for even mentioning
race, poverty, and the fragility of those
under their care.

After an MRI,
I was finally released from the hospital.
We staggered out to the car
and drove away shellshocked,
observing with horror
a homeless man lying facedown
on the sidewalk just a block from the hospital,
his walker still standing upright
by his body.

In this lesser of two cities
there was no refuge,
no mercy to be found for the
wretched of the earth.

Crown of Thorns

I spent days in a prison-like bed,
hemmed in by high, padded siderails
and an alarm set to go off if I left
without a nurse.
Both of my arms were hooked up
to IVs or monitors.
My head was tethered to the
wall behind it
by a cord connected to dozens of
electrodes attached to my
freshly shaven skull,
providing a continuous stream
of images of
brain activity
to a computer monitor
by my enclosure.

At one point, I made the mistake
of looking at myself on the monitor,
and, as Melville said of Ahab,
"There was a crucifixion in his face."

Indeed, after months of taking
what the same old courage teacher called
the "universal thump"
I was humbled, leveled, and
laid as low as I'd ever been.
I too had seen the dark patches
where those lonely, wandering, lost souls
on our streets live every day,
finding no place of solace or refuge,
lurching between terror and rage.

This was my crown of thorns—
not knowing if I'd ever occupy my right mind again,
whether I would ever read, write, or concentrate
with focus.

Would I be set adrift forever?

After days of this, I left the hospital.
Sitting numb and defeated in
the passenger seat,
I was only reached by
the visage of yet another abandoned soul
sitting in a wheelchair
on the street outside the ER,
still wearing a frayed hospital gown,
and holding a sign
that simply said,
"Help."

Stars

Perhaps you won't believe me,
but there were stars behind my eyes
as I sat in meditation
in the darkness of our back room,
listening to the rain pouring down,
baptizing the broken world
and my mind after
weeks of being battered by pain,
sleeplessness, exhaustion, delirium,
seizures, psychotic breaks, and
the haunting memory of the
sheer panic on the faces of my beloveds,
my wife and son, summoning the courage
to weather the storm—
like the beleaguered crew of a
galleon of old,
battening down the hatches,
and securing the deck
as they held on for dear life.

But now, I kept my eyes closed
and my body melted
as the top of my head opened
revealing the vastness of the universe beyond
the stars.
Then I felt, intuited more than saw,
the interconnectedness of all things,
like a loving embrace
that transcended the physical,
but leveled me with awe
and left me stunned by the
thereness of it,

naked, egoless,
not knowing names or
any word that could capture
the essence of it.

As I came back to myself,
eyes still shut,
the stars took on a
a deep glow.
And I remember that it was my wife's face
I was tenderly stroking,
trembling with adoration.
The sound of the rain falling,
drop after drop
on the roof of
our shabby Craftsman house,
splashing the fragile windowpanes,
as the warm breeze
from the tropical storm came in,
all of it blending into a joyous song
that fused with my breath
and became a
deep, resonant humming,
that seeped into the core
of that thing I call me
but is really everything
that is.
And it all started
glowing, glowing, glowing.
Then, when I opened my eyes,
the luminosity persisted,

framing the edges of the windows
and sitting like a crown atop the extended
branches of the bottlebrush tree
swaying outside in the wind.

My wife's face and body were resplendent
as were the richly grained panels of hardwood
in the floor as
I walked down the hallway.
And it continued when I lay down in bed,
the whole world aglow,
dancing with radiance.
As I switched off the light,
the stars were back behind my eyes,
and they lingered there until
I slipped away into emptiness,
smiling.

The Big Dance

for Jeff

In the hospital
I lived at the nexus of life and death,
a place where they danced together,
and held each other tightly in an
intimate embrace.
In the hours before dawn,
as I lay awake listening,
they played a lullaby
when a baby was born on another floor
and this was answered by color-coded alerts
on my ward,
usually indicating an emergency
or the death of someone.
After hearing this jarring juxtaposition regularly,
the lullaby came to summon joy,
while the alerts left me solemn
as I awaited either screams of distress from afar
or hushed silence which was punctured only
by the unmistakable sound of a gurney
bearing the lifeless body of another stranger,
an unknown fellow traveler,
who hadn't made it
down the perilous road back from
an organ transplant or cancer surgery.

Sometimes I would hear the wailing
of a grieving family
and other times,
just the sound of the wheels
creaking as they rolled down
the sterile white hallway
past the nurses at the main desk,

who sat quietly,
as if in silent tribute or
humble acknowledgement of
the limits of their ability
to overcome
the relentless power of death.

I lay there for hours and just listened,
bearing witness.
When I told my son, a cancer survivor,
about these moments
of birth and passing,
and how they came to be part
of the same song,
he said, "There is a certain kind of beauty to it."
And there was.
It was a bittersweet experience
of the celebration and lamentation that is life,
a glimpse into the heart
of the cycle of cessation and becoming
that makes us who we are,
everyday dying, everyday being born.

It reminded me of a piece of jarring yet elegant
avant-garde classical music,
or better yet,
improvisational jazz or rock solos,
where the player seeks to ride the
discordant music of life as it is
with no apologies.
And if they are lucky enough to find it,
they capture,

in a moment of transcendence,
the deep grief, profound wonder, and uncertainty
of our lives.

Lean into it, dear reader—
take it to heart.

Nothing lasts.

That is what the classics I teach
from virtually every culture share
in common—the awful truth of
life's fragility and
the exhortation to savor the mystery
of this very moment.
Right now, say the Buddhists.
Practice excellence in the
pursuit of beauty,
declare the Ancient Greeks,
because we live for but this single transient
passage through time.
Don't waste a second,
even of your youth.
Thus, the wisdom of old
beckons us—*carpe diem,*
seize the day,
your time here is fleeting,
perhaps shorter than you expect.
Then it will be up to others to
remember for you.
The path in front of us
is uncertain and filled with hidden hurdles—

cracks, holes, and fallen trees blocking
the way forward,
but we struggle on and then
one day, hopefully peacefully,
but perhaps with much suffering,
we end.

So, now, while you still can—
think good thoughts, speak good words, and do good deeds—
do one thing well, gently, and with kindness.
Find your way, only you can do it,
one step after another,
for as long as you can.

What Was It Like?

So what was it like,
almost dying?

It was like falling out
of the world,
away from the vast horizons
and the loving embrace
of crowds of beautiful strangers—
the books of their lives
written on their faces—
losing sight of the
gorgeous monsters of cities,
and the paths
that take you away from them
to the shade of old trees
and the greenness of grass
growing amidst
weathered stones.

It was like tumbling away
from myself
into small spaces in rooms—
a spot on a bed,
hours of the false comfort of sheets
and warm covers—
then slowly,
bit by bit,
losing strength, sleep,
good humor,
hunger,
and worst of all,
desire.

It was watching myself recede,
losing grasp of my mind,
my hold over sentences,
the intimate touch of words,
and concentration—
becoming nothing but
breath and sight
and bottomless grief
like falling down a hole
with no way out
as the voices of
my beloveds
grew faint
in the far distance.

It was the blank stillness of night
with only the sound of
my heart pounding fiercely.

It's arriving at a place where
you realize that you control
nothing,
not your body, your emotions, your mind.
Helpless and trembling,
you shiver at the emptiness
at your core,
the realization
that you have no core
but are instead
a dry fallen leaf
floating on the surface of
a restless river,

gliding until you
sink
and are just the river
or really a speck of
the atomic soup
of water
or what we think
is water
rather than merely a part
of the flow of things
beyond time.

Underneath the fear
there is surrender and release.
Not so much ecstasy or joy
but abandon and drift.

You are
simply
not
there.

And how did it feel
to live again?

It was amazement at
the sweetness of apple juice
and the delicious bite of bitter coffee
blended with the sharpness of
a thousand needle pricks
in my arm,
and the feel
of my stapled torso.

It was loving the texture
of all that we feel,
even the mysterious
contours of pain.

It was the touch
of my lover's hand,
the smell of my son's hair
as he bent over me,
the taste of the thick
salt of tears.

It was struggling to sit up,
so weak after losing
sixty pounds in six days,
being helped to eat slowly
and then, most important of all,
to walk,
step after step
on the cold tile floor
of the hospital,
the creaky hardwood
in my house,
and the broken pavement
of the sidewalk outside—
seeing the Mexican poppies
blooming in the yard,
hearing the whiz
and twitter of hummingbirds,
feeling the tender blades of grass
underneath my bare feet.

And, as it went on,
the world came back,
one footstep
at a time—
the families at the taco shop,
neighbors walking dogs,
the huge, unruly Ficus
in the park
where the lawn is full of rabbits at dawn,
hawks soaring across the canyon,
and the ruins of
the fountain
by the pathway
that winds down the hillside
past a sea of orange flowers.

It was holding
my wife's hand in mine
as my gait
became steady,
hearing the dirt crunch
under the soles of my shoes,
knowing that everything we need
is always
right here
in front of us.

Gift

There are some debts one can never repay.
The liver that saved my life
came from a young person
I'm told.
I don't know what befell them—
a sudden unexpected death?
A car crash?
Or some other tragic fate?
I may never know.
The one thing I can imagine
is the deep suffering
of the family
that has to bear the unbearable burden
of an unthinkable loss.

My thoughts are with you,
beloved strangers.

But know this—out of your agony
was born hope for my family—
a husband for my wife of 34 years,
a father for my 19-year-old son.

This is no repayment, to be sure,
but perhaps it is
some small measure of
grace.

This One Small Life

If one day
the blood I spit in the sink
turns out to mean that
I'm dying,
what will this
one small life,
this stream of continuous
moments
that are me
amount to?

As much as we try
to trap ourselves
into a snapshot
in time,
we cannot be measured
or defined by
grief, joy, anger, boredom,
or any of the
myriad moods
that flow through us.

I am not my dying
or becoming,
not agony, ecstasy,
dignity, despair, desire,
pride, envy or humility.
Nor am I triumphant, transcendent,
or absurd—
just all these things
running together
in the flux.

I am made of memories
of running through
the orange groves,
open fields,
rocky hillsides,
green forests,
and sandy beaches
of my childhood.

I am the ballfields,
basketball courts,
grid irons,
grass, dirt, sweat,
and bloody fights
of early contests—
the sound of the baseball
in the glove
and off the bat,
the feel of hitting
and being hit,
the easy grace
and quick movement
of my youthful body,
the sound of sneakers squeaking
on the court,
the basketball leaving my hands
as I leap through
the air.

I am the endless
shelves of books
I've read,
the ocean of words,
phrases, sentences,
and passages pored
over, again and again—
Whitman, Lispector, Neruda,
Kerouac, Thich Nhat Hanh,
Knausgaard, Miller, Kafka,
Duras, Baldwin, Oliver,
and on and on.

All the flashes of insight,
meditative moments,
thoughts that cut
deep and hard,
the beauty that cracked
the shell of myself
and left me exposed
to the black of night
and the glory of
the new day,
the unspeakable brilliance
of stars
and the burning heat
of the sun.

The music too is me—
the sounds that crept
into the forgotten corners
of my being
and grew deep roots there
like the silence between
trumpet notes of Miles Davis,
the lilting rise
of Jerry Garcia's guitar,
slow blues,
tender plaintive voices,
the rush of jubilant, ecstatic noise,
jams, dub, punk, and spare acoustic strumming,
the geometric precision of Bach,
and the forgotten
wonders of melody.

And the art is me—
seeing things just like Robert Frank
on a lonely American highway,
Van Gogh in the garden,
Vermeer peering into the pantry
through a side window.

The funky old houses are me—
Craftsman, Victorian, Spanish style
along with the Modernist landmarks
and the spare lines
that frame the studio
down the street.
I've walked by them all
and every wandering step is made
of longing, curiosity,
and the melancholy light
of a late fall afternoon
in the park.

The millions of footsteps
exploring the insides of buildings,
classrooms, union halls, picket lines,
hotels, and ballparks in cities,
and the open spaces outside them,
under the cover of redwoods by the sea,
across the desert, up alpine trails,
or by farms and patches of wildflowers.

I've seen there the faces of animals,
the gladness and glory
of their movements—
the sweet eyes of deer,
the lumbering carriage of bears,
and the delicate poetry of birdsong.
I love them all and their brethren
are part of me.
I see myself in
the woodland critters and sea creatures—
the grand elk, big horn sheep,
jack rabbits, chipmunks,
turtles, dolphins,
grey whales, starfish, urchins
and snails
along with a host of animals
lost to the world.
I mourn the vanished,
love and remember them
with bittersweet fondness.

What will the world be
without you?

I too am the faces I've kissed,
the breasts suckled,
thighs stroked,
and bodies that have engulfed me.

Is there a more holy place
than where we touch each other
naked and alone together
as our skin tingles,
and flesh engorges and merges
with the other?
I am those intimate caresses
as well as bear hugs,
pats on the back,
hands on shoulders, and
the wonderfully
terrifying moments
when our eyes
lock into each other
and share everything
and more
without words.

I am you, sisters and brothers,
And you are me—
groping from minute to minute,
second by second—
newborn, child, adolescent,
young adult, middle-aged,
old and dying.
I am mother, father, child,
parent, grandparent,
and all those who came before
and will come after
are me,
right now—

staring at the blood in the sink
and knowing it is
our time
but not wanting it to be—
yearning for just one more
perfect fall morning
when there is dawn in me,
one more gentle twilight sky
as I sit on the porch
and lose myself
in the deep glowing red
between the branches
of the grand old pine tree
as cars roll by honking,
ambulances screaming,
and the wings of birds
fluttering above me
like a miracle
as profound as any other
day we have
for as long as we
are still breathing
and deeply adoring the air
that bathes this precious, beautiful,
horrifying, grace-filled world we share.

My blood, your blood,
everyone's blood
flows together
and apart
in unison,

feeding the life
we witness
and hold tenderly
for how long
we don't know.

I just know that
this very instant
has always been
and will always be
so full and
glowing with love
that it blinds us
to see it.

About the Author

Jim Miller is a native San Diegan and a graduate of the MFA program at San Diego State University. In addition to his MFA in Fiction, he has a Ph.D. in American Culture Studies from Bowling Green State University in Ohio. He teaches English, Humanities, and Labor Studies at San Diego City College and lives in San Diego with his wife, Kelly Mayhew, and son, Walter.

Miller is the author of the poetry collection *Paradise and Other Lost Places* (City Works Press, 2024), and his novels include *Last Days in Ocean Beach* (SD City Works Press, 2018), *Flash* (AK Press, 2010), and *Drift* (University of Oklahoma Press, 2007 and 2024). He is also co-author of a history of San Diego, *Under the Perfect Sun: The San Diego Tourists Never See* (with Mike Davis and Kelly Mayhew, The New Press, 2003 and 2005), and a cultural studies book on working class sports fandom, *Better to Reign in Hell: Inside the Raiders Fan Empire* (with Kelly Mayhew, The New Press, 2005). In addition to this he is the editor of *Sunshine/Noir: Writing from San Diego and Tijuana* (City Works Press, 2005), *Sunshine/Noir II: Writing from San Diego and Tijuana* (with Kelly Mayhew, City Works Press, 2015), and *Democracy in Education; Education for Democracy* (AFT 1931, 2007). He has published poetry, fiction, and non-fiction in a wide range of journals and other publications, and, along with Kelly Mayhew and Doug Porter, has a Substack journal called *The Jumping-Off Place* as well as a weekly column in the blog *Words and Deeds,* a monthly column in the *San Diego Union-Tribune's* "Community Voices Project," and he previously wrote for the *San Diego Free Press* and the *OB Rag.*